STEPS TO GET MORE CLIENTS, MORE INCOME AND MORE CONFIDENCE

The Consistency Pill

Alan Browning

TABLE OF CONTENTS

INTRODUCTION

Being a business owner isn't simple, and while every business owner wants to succeed on all fronts, some firms fail. In this book, we'll look at methods to gain more clients, money, and confidence in your business enterprise. These categories will be expanded as you read. Look at this as a journey to more success in your business.

CHAPTER ONE

1.0 Clients

Every owner of a small business wants to draw in new clients. Here are 10 tried-and-true strategies to help you hire "fresh blood."

1.1 Ask for referrals

One of the best ways to gain new clients is through referrals, but if you wait around for your present clients to recommend their friends and relatives to you, it can take a while. Take control by putting in place a procedure for aggressively requesting recommendations from your delighted clients. Include activities that generate referrals in the sales process. Send a follow-up email, for instance, asking for a recommendation after a customer has received a purchase from your online store. When your business-to-business salespeople contact customers to provide answers to questions following a sale, have them ask for referrals.

(Never be afraid to ask for referral)

<u>*1.2 Network*</u>

Participate in networking groups and events that are pertinent to your market and your clients to generate some good old-fashioned word of mouth. Don't approach networking with a "what's in it for me" mentality; instead, ask yourself, "How can I help others?" Finding customers should be about solving their problems to create a solid network.

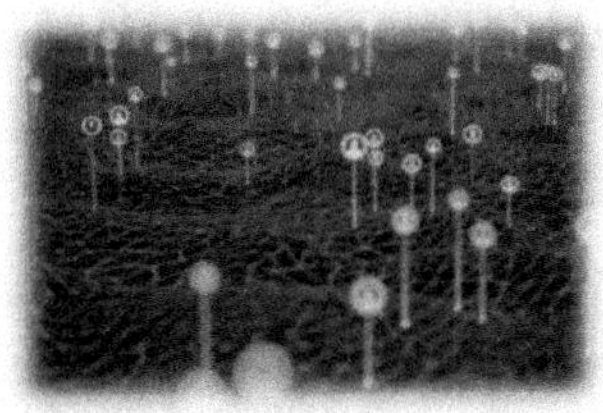

(Build that network)

<u>*1.3 Offer discounts and incentives for new customers only*</u>

Introductory deals, like a two-week karate lesson at your studio for $100, might entice potential clients by giving them a risk-free option to explore your goods or services. Monitor the clientele that always make use of promo deals and send them advertisements to promote continued patronage of the business.

1.4 Re-contact old customers

Everything old can be made new again, even if a customer hasn't bought from you in a while. Regularly review your client connections, and after six months or a year without a conversation or transaction, engage dormant consumers by phone, email, or direct mail with a unique offer. They'll be grateful that you thought of them and will try to win you back.

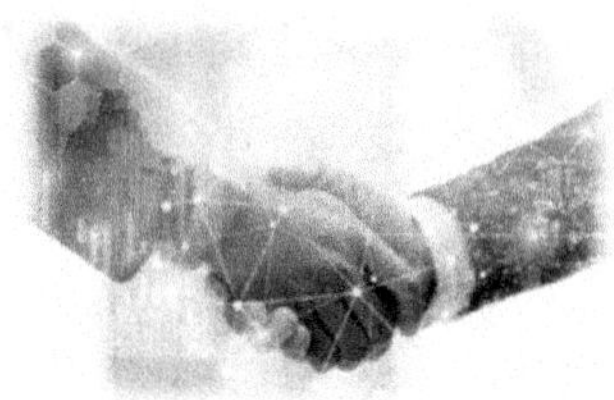

(Don't lose contact with your old customers)

1.5 Improve your website

Online searches are now the primary way that both consumers and business to business buyers find new businesses. This means that in order to draw in new clients, your website must work really hard. Check your website quickly to make sure the layout, text, photos, and search engine optimization are up to date. If this isn't your area of expertise, it would be wise to hire a website design company and/or a search engine optimization expert.

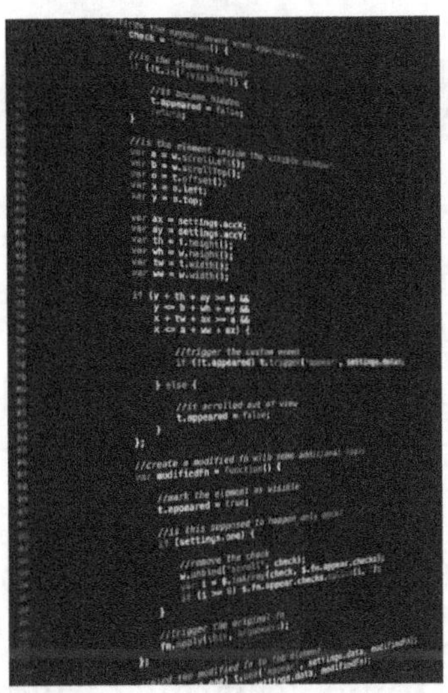

(Design a good website for consumers)

1.6 Partner with complementary businesses

Plan how you can target each other's clients to bring in new business by collaborating with companies who serve comparable clientele but aren't directly competitors. A maternity clothing website and a website for baby supplies, for instance, can collaborate to give deals and discounts to each other's customers.

(Collaborate with like-minded businesses)

1.7 Promote your expertise

By promoting your sector knowledge, you can attract attention—and new clients. Your subject expertise will be displayed by taking part in industry panel discussions or online webinars, speaking at industry events or to groups your target clients belong to, or holding educational sessions or workshops.

Do customers provide reviews for your company online? Cultivate your reviews to make the most of them. Promote Yelp reviews on your website and in-store signs to encourage people to do so (or wherever the reviews are). Since social proof is so powerful, new customers are more likely to try your business if they witness others praising it.

(Make use of your online reviews)

1.9 Participate in community events

Generally speaking, people prefer to support locally owned businesses in their neighborhoods. Participate in community outreach programs and organizations to raise your profile. Sponsor a neighborhood 5K, plan a holiday "gifts for kids" drive, or buy equipment for a local Little League team. This will make your company well-known and draw in potential customers.

(Community events help draw in potential customers)

1.10 Bring a friend

Offer 2-for-1, "buy one, get one free," or "bring a friend" discounts to encourage your "regulars" to bring in new clients. A restaurant might, for instance, conduct a "buy one entrée, get the second for free" promotion to entice additional patrons. Invite a buddy to sample our newest happy hour discounts! You might even be more specific to let them know that you wish to grow the clientele for your business.

<u>*1.11 Have a clearly defined niche*</u>

A business niche is a certain segment of a larger market that your company specializes in or focuses on. Finding a specialty sets your company apart from the competition and enables you to dominate your industry. You can understand the significance of choosing your expertise and standing out from the competition if you've ever heard the saying "jack of all trades, master of none." Small business entrepreneurs who desire a passive source of revenue and devoted clients must choose a niche/gap that they can fill.

(A niche must be found before a business)

CHAPTER TWO

2.0 Income

You can grow your business by looking for new markets or sales tactics. To increase sales, you may need to expand your market, strengthen your marketing efforts, launch new products or services, or improve customer service. If you're a manufacturer, this may imply increasing output to meet demand.

2.1 Introduce new products or service

Provide your customers with a broader range of goods or services. You must undertake market research to establish whether there is a demand for your proposed offering. Consider using some of your existing clients as a test group. By gathering input from a test group, you can eliminate some of the risks and learn how to improve the product or service. Consider marketing and promotion of your new products and services to ensure that people are aware of them.

(Introducing new products won't hurt)

2.2 *Expand to new domestic markets*

Despite entering new markets can be costly, it can help you develop your audience. With the help of market research, you may design a strategy and have a deeper understanding of the potential new market. To meet the new demand, you'll also need to consider marketing, sales, distribution, and increasing production.

(Expanding in your residing area is always a good idea)

2.3 *Enhance your sales channels*

By examining and enhancing your sales channels, you may be able to increase market domination, expand your clientele, and increase profitability. As an example, you could:

- Improve your sales team's training.
- Add retail sites by recruiting resellers or enlisting independent sales people.
- Create an internet business plan.

2.4 *Marketing activities*

You might be able to improve the effectiveness of your marketing efforts. Keep an eye on the results of your present marketing or advertising efforts and be prepared to change your plan if needed. Analyze the most effective methods for reaching your target demographic and modify your marketing plan accordingly.

(Marketing ensures your product is known)

<u>*2.5 Change your price*</u>

Changing your tariffs, terms, or billing criteria may improve market demand for your goods and services. Be mindful of what your competitors are offering and your own profit margins to determine if you can cut costs. If you can't lower your prices, you can frequently convince clients by offering a better deal with better terms.

(Change your price to favor you)

<u>*2.6 Be aware of the competition*</u>

Always keep an eye out for what your competitors are up to. With this knowledge, you can better understand their behaviors, skills, and restrictions. Knowing this will help you defend your market position, adjust to changes, and uncover new markets.

2.7 Improve community relations
Increase your visibility and presence in your neighborhood. You can raise client awareness and sales by participating in activities such as sponsoring neighborhood events, giving speeches, and supporting a local sports team.

2.9 Don't neglect customer service
Consider how your customers may assess the effectiveness or responsiveness of your customer service. A delighted customer's positive word of mouth benefits your company.

2.10 Know when to stop
It may be time to abandon any markets, services, or product lines with low profit margins or excessive selling costs. Getting rid of less profitable items or services can be difficult if you are dedicated to your current offerings, but doing so can save you money and allow for more strategic reinvestment.

<u>*2.11 Learn a high-end skill*</u>
It assists in providing you with informed new perspectives on the environment around you. Your neural connections are kept active, you are exposed to new experiences, and your brain is educated to deal with a wide range of difficulties. These components operate in tandem to keep you healthy. This could eventually result in a high-end tool to help your business.

(Build your arsenal of skills to be relevant)

CHAPTER THREE

3.0 Confidence

In addition to advancing your professional development and skills, the following tactics offer ways to assist you increase your working confidence:

3.1 Attend professional development training

Increasing the talents, you need for your career can have an effect on your level of confidence in general. When you raise your level of expertise or further develop a particular skill, like learning a new coding language if you work in IT, you can perform better in your profession, which can boost your confidence. Attend professional development or skills training, if possible. To learn new project management techniques, for instance, you may enroll in a class or attend a training session. You might also study journals or books to get the knowledge you need to advance your credentials.

(Development training will give you skills you'll be proud of!)

3.2 Learn new skills

Learning whole new abilities or furthering your education can have a significant impact on your overall confidence, much like honing your current skills does. By enabling you to evaluate your abilities and drive to learn more, choosing to exercise your development can help you feel more confident. When you learn a new talent, you can use it at work to improve your productivity, your capacity for maintaining organization, and your ability to take on new jobs with greater assurance.

3.3 Dress for success

Improve your job appearance to fit the standards of the workplace by taking into account your professional clothing. If your workplace has a "business casual" dress code, for example, wear a pair of casual slacks rather than denim jeans. You might feel more confident performing your job and engaging with peers and superiors if you dress more professionally and present yourself professionally when you arrive at work. In a similar vein, refrain from wearing casual clothing to formal business attire for significant occasions like conferences, board meetings, or other presentations.

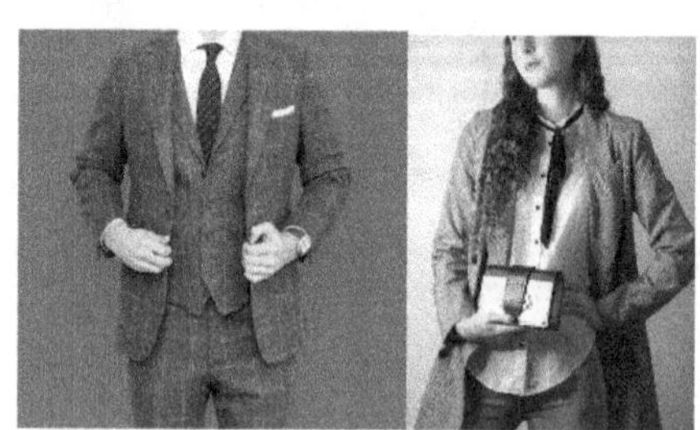

(Responsible dressing helps your self-image)

3.4 Leave your comfort zone

Although stepping outside of your comfort zone can be one of the most effective strategies to build your confidence, it can also be difficult to do. For example, if giving presentations in front of the entire sales and marketing team has always been something you despise. You may challenge yourself by offering to make the next presentation or partnering up with a coworker to host. If this is the case, you should prepare your presentation. You would completely move outside of your comfort zone, but concentrating on your abilities, the presentation itself, and how you would give it rather than the mistakes you might make or worrying about shame would help you overcome that fear and generally enhance your job confidence. Taking a risk can also open up chances that you might have missed otherwise. For instance, continuing with your presentation can offer a new opportunity for promotion or client acquisition that, had you stayed in your comfort zone, you might have missed.

(Self confidence can't be grown in a shell)

3.5 Emulate confident peers

Think about the successful people you know, or look for someone who exudes confidence and self-assurance in their work, and pay attention to their demeanor and social interactions. You can boost your personal confidence by employing some of the strategies used by your confident colleagues in their work lives.

(Confidence begets confidence)

3.6 Set goals for yourself

Setting both short-term and long-term job goals might affect how you view your accomplishments and talents. Consider setting a goal for yourself to improve your overall abilities or master a new skill. You can quantify your achievement even further by focusing on tiny targets that will help you get to your desired result. If you examine each minor triumph, you achieve while working toward a larger goal, you will be able to identify how you are employing successful tactics to improve your development. You might decide to boost your total work productivity, for instance. Then, you can establish more manageable goals to assist you get there, such as developing better time management techniques or concentrating on one activity at a time rather than multitasking. You can increase your confidence in your ability to do your job well as you achieve each achievement along the way to your objective of boosting productivity.

(Achieved goals produce a confident mind)

3.7 Focus on your strengths

By forcing you to assess your success and ability, concentrating on your strengths can give you more confidence. Professionals who put in a lot of effort to improve their job usually focus too much on little slip-ups or blunders rather than the overall success of the endeavor. If this is the case, making a list of your characteristics and skills, as well as another list of your successes, may assist to reduce this tendency. You can make it a routine to read them each morning and whenever you need a confidence boost throughout the day.

(Perfecting known strengths builds self-confidence)

3.8 Learn from your mistakes
When executing improvement plans and goal-setting techniques, mistakes are frequently unavoidable. The secret is to analyze your errors and extract lessons from them. Although accepting failure can be challenging, it can affect how you use your abilities in subsequent trials. For instance, you might have formatted the code for a data entry program wrong,

but rather than realizing your error and beginning over, you might check the place where you typed the defective code to determine whether you made a casual error or if the code in question was faulty. By using the knowledge, you gained via self-reflection to make the error right, you can then learn from this misstep.

(Have no regrets about mistakes)

3.9 Eliminate negative language

Taking an honest look at how you see yourself might also help you gain confidence. You can take efforts to alter your thinking if you discover that you frequently doubt yourself or are overly critical of yourself. You may try self-affirming activities like reflecting on all your recent victories or listing the professional traits you most value in yourself in a notebook. Continue to assess the beneficial professional advancements you have made, and keep rewarding yourself when you finish tasks to your manager's satisfaction or higher standards.

(Negative language will only bring you down)

3.10 Ask questions

You can increase your self-confidence in your career by being assertive in your self-learning and asking questions. During team meetings, project planning sessions, or conferences, think about making it a practice to ask at least one question to assist clarify any information that could otherwise be unclear to you. When you do this regularly as part of your work routine, you can boost your emotions of confidence and self-worth via participation. This can demonstrate to your team mates and superiors that you will take initiative when you believe you might need additional direction. Similar to this, you might have coworkers who are trying to gain confidence. By taking the initiative to speak up and ask questions, you might allay their fears.

(Question asking will help your self-esteem)

3.11 Tips for implementing confidence-building strategies

The following advice can help you stay on your successful path while you seek to increase your job confidence.

3.11.1 *Take your time*

With your efforts and ambitions for professional development, take your time and practice patience. Set realistic deadlines for completing your tasks on your plan. You might also think about utilizing a spreadsheet or checklist to keep track of your progress.

3.11.2 *Be persistent*

Alter might take time; therefore, you might discover that your goals need to be modified to take into account any conditions that change. You can guarantee that you maintain making progress toward boosting your confidence, though, by being persistent in your actions and improvement plans.

3.11.3 *Keep developing your mindset*

Self-reflection and assessment can both benefit from having a growth mindset because it establishes a baseline for how you view yourself. In the job, accepting challenges, conquering difficulties, and celebrating your achievements can boost your confidence.

CHAPTER FOUR

4.0 Conclusion

Now that you've reached the end of this book, consider the content shared on how to increase clients, income, and confidence. These categories covered topics such as networking, asking for referrals, changing your price, learning a high-end skill, eliminating negative language, and learning from your mistakes etc. If you adhere to these guidelines, you can expect adequate results. Hopefully by the end of this book you have gained the necessary tools to make your business succeed now go and make money!!!!!!!